PEOPLE WHO HELP
ANIMALS

By JANET PREUS

Illustrated by CHARLOTTE COOKE & DAN CRISP

CANTATA
LEARNING
MANKATO, MINNESOTA

WWW.CANTATALEARNING.COM

**CANTATA
LEARNING**
MANKATO, MINNESOTA

Published by Cantata Learning
1710 Roe Crest Drive
North Mankato, MN 56003
www.cantatalearning.com

Library of Congress Control Number: 2014957015
978-1-63290-268-9 (hardcover/CD)
978-1-63290-420-1 (paperback/CD)
978-1-63290-462-1 (paperback)

People Who Help Animals by Janet Preus
Illustrated by Charlotte Cooke

Book design, Tim Palin Creative
Editorial direction, Flat Sole Studio
Executive musical production and direction, Elizabeth Draper
Music arranged and produced by Steven C Music

Printed in the United States of America.

VISIT
WWW.CANTATALEARNING.COM/ACCESS-OUR-MUSIC
TO SING ALONG TO THE SONG

Animals live all around us.

We keep them as pets. Some we see in zoos. But most animals live in the **wild**. There are people who work to keep animals healthy and safe. Come meet some of the people who help animals.

Now turn the page, and sing along.

Let's begin with a veterinarian.
She's also called a "vet."

She's an animal doctor with special **medicine**
that's just right for your pet.

There are people who help the pets that we adore,
and people helping the animals that live outdoors.

At the zoo you can see **exotic** animals like leopards and kangaroos.

A zookeeper works to keep them **healthy**, and he feeds them too.

There are people who help the pets
that we adore,
and people helping the animals
that live outdoors.

A cat is outside and meowing in the night.
He must be lost and all alone.

An **animal shelter** worker feeds the cat
and finds him a new home.

There are people who help the pets
that we adore,
and people helping the animals
that live outdoors.

A bear roams around a neighbor's backyard.

That's not where he should be.

So a **conservation officer** gives him a ride

to a field full of sweet berries.

There are people who help the pets
that we adore,
and people helping the animals
that live outdoors.

SONG LYRICS
People Who Help Animals

Let's begin with a veterinarian.
She's also called a "vet."

She's an animal doctor with
  special medicine
that's just right for your pet.

There are people who help the pets
that we adore,
and people helping the animals
that live outdoors.

At the zoo you can see exotic animals
like leopards and kangaroos.

A zookeeper works to keep them healthy,
and he feeds them too.

There are people who help the pets
that we adore,
and people helping the animals
that live outdoors.

A cat is outside and meowing in
  the night.
He must be lost and all alone.

An animal shelter worker feeds the cat
and finds him a new home.

There are people who help the pets
that we adore,
and people helping the animals
that live outdoors.

A bear roams around a neighbor's
  backyard.
That's not where he should be.
So a conservation officer gives him a ride
to a field full of sweet berries.

There are people who help the pets
that we adore,
and people helping the animals
that live outdoors.

People Who Help Animals

Steven C Music

1. Let's be-gin with a veter-i-nar-i-an. She's al-so called a "vet."

She's an an-i-mal doc-tor with spe-cial med-i-cine that's just right for your pet.

Chorus

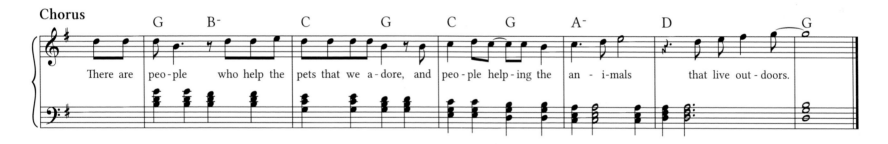

There are peo-ple who help the pets that we a-dore, and peo-ple help-ing the an-i-mals that live out-doors.

Verse 2
At the zoo you can see exotic animals
like leopards and kangaroos.
A zookeeper works to keep them healthy,
and he feeds them too.

Chorus

Verse 3
A cat is outside and meowing in the night.
He must be lost and all alone.
An animal shelter worker feeds the cat
and finds him a new home.

Chorus

Verse 4
A bear roams around a neighbor's backyard.
That's not where he should be.
So a conservation officer gives him a ride
to a field full of sweet berries.

Chorus

GLOSSARY

animal shelter—a place that gives animals food and a place to stay until they find a new home

conservation officer—a person who helps protect wildlife

exotic—different or strange

healthy—fit and well, not sick

medicine—a substance used to help sick or injured people get better

wild—a natural setting not controlled by people

GUIDED READING ACTIVITIES

1. Who is the author of this book? Why do you think she titled this book *People Who Help Animals*?

2. Do you have a pet? Who are the people that help your pet stay safe and healthy?

3. Draw a picture of your favorite animal in this book.

TO LEARN MORE

Clendening, John. *Animal Shelters.* New York: PowerKids Press, 2015.

Markarian, Margie. *Who Scoops Elephant Poo?* Chicago: Raintree, 2011.

Meister, Cari. *Veterinarians*. Minneapolis: Bullfrog Books, 2015.

Townsend, John. *Amazing Animal Helpers*. Chicago: Raintree, 2013.